100 Great Literacy Ideas

Using AccuCut® Dies

Written by Elaine Haven, M.S. Ed.

Editor	Kindra Foster
Graphic Design and Layout	Lynn Gibney
Photography	Ryan Ninete
Project Stylists	AccuCut Design Department

ISBN 0-9710829-4-4

100 Great Literacy Ideas Using AccuCut® Dies
Copyright 2004 by AccuCut Systems, a division of TEK Industries, Inc.
All die designs ©1999-2004 by AccuCut Systems.
1035 E. Dodge Street, Fremont, NE 68025
800-288-1670/402-721-4134
www.accucut.com

Table of Contents

For an alphabetical list of dies used in projects...see the inside back cover!

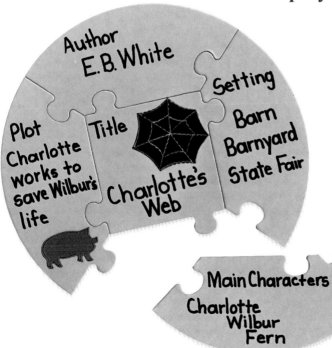

More 100 Great Ideas Books

Dear AccuCut Customer:

We realize your time is precious. AccuCut works hard to help you save time by providing die-cut shapes that match your curriculum needs and make learning more meaningful for students!

This book, *100 Great Literacy Ideas Using AccuCut® Dies*, is the third in a series of exciting curriculum idea books from AccuCut. The books show you how to engage students in learning with hands-on activities using die cuts. They include a wealth of ideas for elementary teachers that encompass brain-based learning techniques— simple enough to integrate into your lesson plans, and effective for all types of learners.

AccuCut's other idea books are packed with versatile learning activities to use in all areas of curriculum. Order your copies today for only $9.99 each!

Available Now:

- *100 Great Math Ideas Using AccuCut Dies*

- *100 Great Game Ideas Using AccuCut Dies*

Available Later in 2004:

- *100 Great Bookmaking Ideas Using AccuCut Dies*

- *100 Great Holiday Ideas Using AccuCut Dies*

- *100 Great Nursery Rhyme & Fairy Tale Ideas Using AccuCut Dies*

Hints & Important Techniques

Clear Cuts™ See-Through Dies Save Time!

Acrylic Clear Cuts™ dies are see-through, so you can position photos, artwork, text, graphic designs and more exactly as you would like to within the shape—so no part of the design gets cut

off. Clear Cuts™ dies make it possible to computer print text for projects, then see exactly where the text fits within the shape, just by looking through the clear part of the die. Clear Cuts dies save you time and assure that your projects look their best! Here's how it works:

Step 1

Place a photo or other item face down on the foam side of a Clear Cuts die. Center the photo in the see-through area of the die.

Step 2

Place the Clear Cuts die with foam side up on the die tray and roll through the AccuCut machine. To remove photo, simply put a finger through the hole in the die and push the photo out.

AccuCut® dies are interchangeable with all brands of hand operated die cutting machines—guaranteed!

Important Techniques

Laminate First, Then Cut

Lamination helps protect the die cut games you make, so you can use them over and over in your classroom! It's best to laminate the paper first, then use a die to cut the desired shape with the AccuCut Roller Die Cutting Machine. If you use a hot laminator, be sure to laminate the paper with at least 3.0-mil lamination plastic, so the plastic doesn't come off of the paper after die cutting. The thicker the lamination film, the better it adheres to the paper.

Cold laminators, such as the Xyron® machine, work best when die cutting shapes, because they use adhesive—no worries about the lamination not melting enough to adhere, as with heat laminators. Call AccuCut at 800-288-1670 for more information about Xyron products.

Cut Patterns or Prints Face Down

For best results, always place paper or other material pattern-side-down on die, then cut using the die cutting machine.

Using the Computer to Make Learning Aids

Although handwritten words are fast, easy and personal, printing the words on your project can lend a polished look that sometimes is preferable. To create die-cut learning aids using computer fonts, first type the words on the computer, estimating the size and position to fit the shape. Print, then position a die cut over the printout to see if the text fits. Adjust as needed to make the text fit. Print the words on colored paper. If desired, laminate before cutting (see tips above). Place the printed sheet print-side-down on the die. Lift up and peek underneath to line up the words before cutting. Clear Cuts see-through acrylic dies allow you to see exactly where the print will appear (see Clear Cuts information at left).

Experiment…and use your imagination to make many different kinds of die-cut projects.

Beginning Reading Activities

1.

Shape Word Wall   *Grades Pre-K – 3*

Create a word wall using color words, number words, sight words or words from students' reading books. Write the words on large or jumbo die-cut stars or other shapes, then attach to a bulletin board or the classroom wall.

Colorful die cuts draw students' attention to words on the wall. Encourage them to use these words when they are writing!

2.

Beanbag Toss   *Grades Pre-K – 1*

Play this game indoors or outdoors. Cut out a variety of letters and die-cut shapes (e.g., cow, fish, pig, butterfly). In a small area, lay the letters and shapes on the floor or ground. Make a line where students will stand. Students stand behind the line and take turns throwing beanbags onto letters and shapes. If the beanbag lands on a shape, the student will say another word that starts with the same beginning sound. If the beanbag lands on a letter, the student will say a word that begins with that letter.

Use this game to study other concepts, too. For example, to teach vowel sounds, put the letters a, e, i, o and u onto the floor, along with shapes beginning with vowel sounds. When the beanbag lands on a vowel or shape, ask students to say the short vowel sound, then say a word beginning with that vowel sound.

100 Great Literacy Ideas Using AccuCut® Dies

3.

Where Are My Reading Glasses? **Grades Pre-K – 2**

Allow each student to decorate a pair of die-cut eyeglasses with mini die cuts, such as flowers, fish, geometric shapes, happy faces and other shapes. Children enjoy reading with their self-designed "reading glasses!"

Idea

Make yourself a pair of die-cut teacher's "reading glasses," and use them when you read a story to the class.

4.

Create a Skit **Grades 2 – 3**

Cut out masks and help second-grade or third-grade students create skits in small groups of three or four. They will write the skits using characters that correspond to the masks they choose. Young children can act out the story as you read it.

Ideas

AccuCut® Masks:

- Bunny
- Cat
- Dog
- Lamb
- Pig
- Bear
- Ladybug

5.

Introducing New Letter Sounds
Grades Pre-K – K

Use masks when you introduce new letters in preschool and kindergarten (e.g., B or b for bunny or bear, D or d for dog). Seeing other students wear masks holding corresponding letters helps students remember the letters.

6.

Word Family Flash Card Wheel
Grades K – 2

AccuCut offers two different flash card wheels. The difference is that Flash Card Wheel #1 has an outer wheel smaller than the inner wheel; Flash Card Wheel #2 is the opposite (an inner wheel smaller than the outer wheel).

To make this project, cut out both parts of a jumbo Flash Card Wheel #1 or Flash Card Wheel #2 and put them together with a brad. On the outside wheel (with the window), write the title "Word Family." Cut off the perforated flap of the window. On the right side of the window, write a word family ending (e.g., "at"). On the inside wheel, write letters that show through the window (e.g., m, b, c, h). When students turn the wheel, it makes words by combining the letter with the ending (i.e., mat, bat, cat, hat).

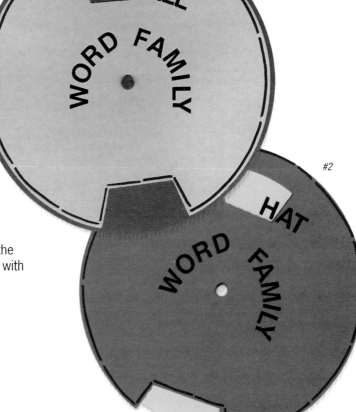

Hint

Include some letters that make nonsense words when combined with the word family ending (e.g., lat, gat, jat). Students love sounding out silly words!

7.

Monkey Words   *Grades Pre-K – 3*

Make a game for a center with AccuCut's monkey Cup Huggers™ die cut. Cut one monkey for each of a number of paper cups for sorting. Wrap a monkey around each cup, and put a label on the front (e.g., capital "A", small "a", "Long Vowels", "Short Vowels"). Create strips using the one-inch Strip Maker die, and write words or letters on them.

Students take turns reading words and letters and then placing them into the correct cup. Write answers on the backs of the monkeys so students can empty cups and check answers.

Ideas

Use the monkey Cup Huggers™ die cut to teach these concepts:

- Rhyming words
- Syllables
- Nouns, verbs, adjectives, adverbs
- Proper nouns/common nouns
- Singular/plural
- Compound words

Other AccuCut Cup Huggers™ shapes include a clown, cowboy, cowgirl, Rover, Santa and snowman. Decorate the generic Cup Huggers shape to look like anyone!

8.

Reading Bookmark *Grades Pre-K – 3*

Cut out the word "READ". It may be used as a bookmark on its own, or it may be glued to Bookmark-Generic #2 or Bookmark-Generic #3. Students enjoy making their own bookmarks for school or home.

THINGS THAT ARE GREEN

9.

Brainstorming *Grades Pre-K – 3*

Ask students to look around the room for items that fit a brainstorming category such as "Things that are green." At the top of a piece of chart paper, write any category of your choice, then glue die-cut shapes of things in that category (e.g., frog, lily pad, pine tree, grass, leaf). Ask students to point out things in the classroom that are green and add them to the list.

Ideas

Use the brainstorming chart and die cuts to complete a number of different brainstorming lists on different days. Here are a few ideas:

- Things that are red
- Things that come in 2's, 3's, 4's, 5's
- Things in which we travel
- Things that grow
- Animals
- Articles of clothing

100 Great Literacy Ideas Using AccuCut® Dies

10.

Story Props Grades Pre-K – 3

Story props created with die cuts make listening to a story more fun and memorable for students. Use a variety of die cuts to create props for any story. Using the book *Elmer,* as an example, cut one jumbo Elephant #2 from gray paper and another elephant from bright patterned paper. Cut out one elephant for each student from white paper. After reading the story, each student may create his or her own unique design on the elephant. On the backs of their elephants they can write one thing that makes them special.

Elmer goes for a long walk in the jungle.

Write different parts of a story on Puzzle Piece #1 die cuts. Ask students to put the story's events in sequential order.

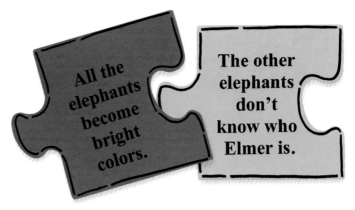

All the elephants become bright colors.

The other elephants don't know who Elmer is.

Elmer makes the other elephants laugh.

Elmer shouts BOO!

Elmer rolls in berries and turns gray.

11.

Story Apron   Grades Pre-K – 2

Purchase or make a fleece apron with deep front pockets to use as a story apron. Cut felt shapes representing characters from a story, and store them in the front pockets of the apron. As you read the story, place the felt shapes onto the apron. After students listen to the story, encourage them to take turns wearing the apron and retelling the story. Retelling increases comprehension and helps develop fluency.

12.

Solve the Puzzle   Grades 1 – 2

Write words on small or large puzzle pieces—one word per piece. Put the words together to make sentences. For a center activity, prepare enough puzzle pieces for five sentences.

For accountability, ask students to write sentences on a piece of paper. As an additional activity, ask the students to mix up the puzzle pieces and make more sentences!

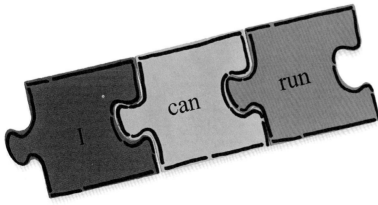

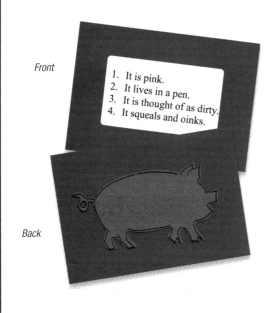

Front

1. It is pink.
2. It lives in a pen.
3. It is thought of as dirty.
4. It squeals and oinks.

Back

13.

Guess What I Have   **Grades Pre-K – 3**

Cut a variety of large die-cut shapes (e.g., pig, fish, flower). Glue the shapes to the backs of large index cards, or use the rectangle inside of a 5" x 7" photo mat die cut. Hold up one card at a time. Ask students to listen to a list of word clues, guess what is on the back of each card, then raise their hands when they think they know the answer.

14.

Phonics Clothesline   **Grades K – 1**

Cut 25 jumbo T-shirts, and write a different vowel on five of them. Decide if you want to use long or short vowel sounds. On the remaining T-shirts, glue pictures of things that begin with the vowel sounds you are teaching.

Hang a string or length of yarn under the blackboard as if it were a clothesline. Put a basket of clothespins on the floor near the clothesline. Students take turns hanging one vowel T-shirt on the line, then all the shirts with pictures whose names include that sound. Then, they hang the next vowel sound T-shirt and continue in the same way. Students can check the backs of the T-shirts when they finish to make sure they have the correct answers.

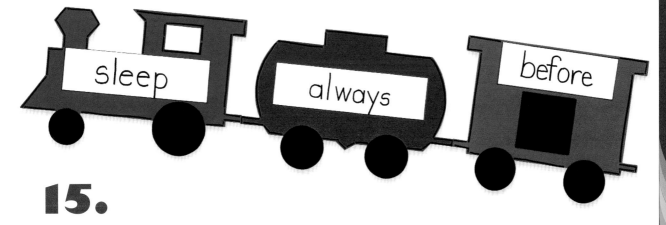

15.

Train Words   *Grades K – 2*

Cut jumbo trains in different colors, plus one caboose. Every day for two weeks, on a train die cut, write a new word you want to introduce to the class. After learning the new word, add it to the train. Students practice the words every day as the train grows. On the last day, put the new word on a caboose. You can store these words for use later in the year!

16.

Spinning Wheels Grades K – 3

For each spinning wheel you want to make, cut one jumbo and one large inner wheel using the large and jumbo Flash Card Wheel die sets. The inner wheel shape in both sizes includes 10 perforated sections. Cut the two wheels from two different colors of paper. Attach the large wheel to the jumbo wheel with a brad. Write letters, words or numbers in the perforated spaces of one wheel and matching information in random spaces on the other wheel.

Students turn the large wheel to match the jumbo wheel. For example: Turn the large wheel section that says "could not" until it is opposite the jumbo wheel section that says "couldn't".

Ideas

Use Spinning Wheels in a center with a variety of different topics, such as:

- Capital/lowercase letters
- Contractions
- Singular to plural
- Color words to color
- Number words to numbers

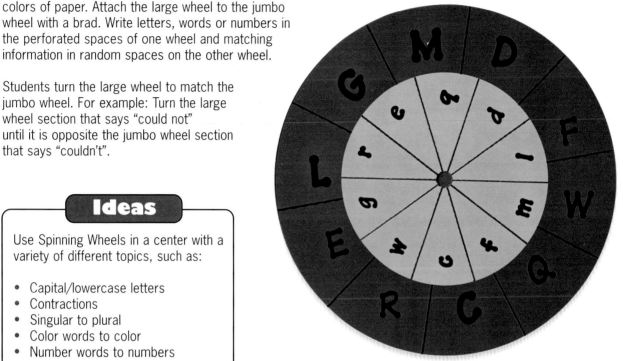

17.

Pigs Help Us Read Grades 1 – 3

On 10 jumbo die-cut pigs, write sight words, spelling words, words from a story, number words or color words. Punch a hole in each pig near its tail. Insert a brad through the holes to attach all the pigs together. Students turn the pigs on the brad and read each word. Older students can use the pigs to practice spelling.

18.

Look At This Grades Pre-K – 2

Cut a large star and glue it onto the end of a tongue depressor. As you or your students read from a chart or the blackboard, use the star pointer to direct their attention. Younger students can use the mini star on a wooden craft stick to follow along in their reading.

19.

Roll Out the Letters Grades K – 1

Attach a piece of adding machine tape to a cardboard tube with tape or glue. Cut out the letters of the alphabet, plus a set of die-cut shapes that begin with each sound (e.g., A and "apple", B and "bear", C and "cat", D and "duck").

Students glue letters and pictures onto the roll, drawing a line across the tape after each letter and picture set. When finished, roll the tape onto the cardboard tube. Students unroll the roll to practice identifying the letters and the sound each letter makes. When they are finished practicing, they roll it back up and attach a paper clip to the roll before storing.

Hint

You don't have to go through the whole alphabet. You can use just the letters you have introduced so far, and let students add to the roll as you add more letters. Or you can use only vowel letters, plus pictures of things that begin with or contain those vowel letter sounds.

NUMBER WORDS

One

Two

Three

Four

Five

Six

Seven

Eight

Nine

Ten

20.

Display of Numbers *Grades Pre-K – 1*

Use die cuts to create a display of numbers to help students practice reading number words and counting. On a piece of chart paper, write a title at the top, such as "Number Words." Write actual number words in a column on the left side of the paper. To the right of the number word, glue small or mini die cuts onto the chart paper to match the number word on the left.

21.

Roll-A-Word

Grades K – 2

Cut two jumbo cubes for each game, one blue and one green. On each face of the blue cube, write a consonant letter that begins a word. On each face of the green cube, write a word ending (e.g., as, at, ip, in, op, on). Assemble the cubes.

Give each student a piece of paper on which to write answers. Working in pairs, the first student rolls the dice. On the paper, he or she writes the word made from the letters on the dice. The second student rolls and writes a word. When each student has completed a number of rolls, students take turns reading their words. They cross out any combinations that are not real words.

Idea

Second graders and more able first graders can play the same game with the first die faces showing digraphs or blends (e.g., sh, th, sl, ch) and digraph endings (e.g., ate, op, at, ip).

22.

Letter of the Week

Grades Pre-K – K

Give each student a colored piece of 9" x 12" construction paper, plus one uppercase and one lowercase letter of the week (e.g., D and d). Cut out shapes that begin with the letter (e.g., dog, dress, duck, dragon, dinosaur), and give to students.

Students glue the letters onto their papers. Go through the die-cut shapes one at a time, and ask students to glue onto the paper the shapes whose names begin with that letter. Make a letter page, also, and post it on the board for students to practice. Remind students to practice the letter when they take it home.

23.

Who Has the Picture Card?

Grades K – 1

Create a set of index cards using the inside of photo mat 5" x 7", and distribute one card to each student in the class. Half of the cards should show a letter, and half of them should show a die-cut shape whose name begins with one of those letters.

Students can sit in a circle or remain in their seats for this activity. Call on two students who have letter cards. Each student must say the letter, then walk around the room and look for the one student who has the shape that matches the letter. When the match is found, the student raises his or her hand and waits for the teacher to ask what the picture is. If the student doesn't find the correct picture, the teacher asks the student who has that picture to stand up and continue the game in the same manner, looking for a match.

24.

Visual Memory   **Grades Pre-K – 2**

Working with the teacher in a small group, students look at a picture created from a variety of die-cut shapes and try to remember the shapes in the picture. The teacher covers up the picture and asks the students questions about what was in the picture.

Idea

Sample questions might be:

a) What animal was in the middle of the picture?
b) What color was that animal?
c) What shape was at the top of the picture?
d) How many stars did you see?
e) What color were those stars?

25.

Pass the Hat I *Grades K – 1*

Cut out the 26 letters of the alphabet, then glue them onto index cards or use the inside rectangle from the photo mat 5" x 7" die. Put all of the letter cards into a hat. Students pass the hat to one another, one student at a time. Each student pulls out a letter, names the letter, then names a word that begins with that letter. Ask the rest of the class to come up with more words that begin with that letter. The hat is then passed to another student.

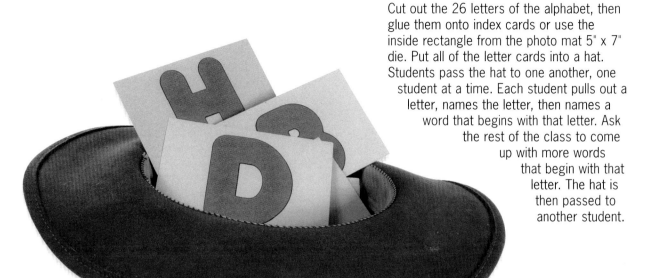

26.

Pass the Hat II *Grades K – 3*

In this activity, instead of cutting out letters, cut shapes whose names begin with different letters (e.g., turkey, flower, cheese, mouse). Glue the shapes onto index cards. Students pass the hat to one another, one student at a time, and each student pulls out a shape card, then names the shape. The student names another word that begins with the same sound, and the class adds to this list. The hat is then passed to the next student.

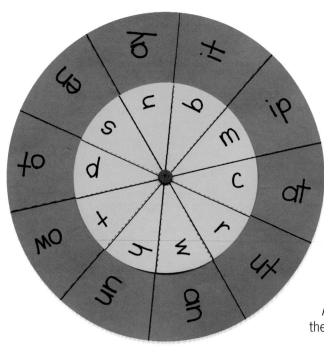

27.

Wheel Games Grades K – 2

Create wheel games for students to use in a center: cut out just the inner wheel of the large and jumbo Flash Card Wheel shapes. This is the part of the wheel with 10 perforated sections. Join the two inner wheels with a brad and write a consonant in each section of the smaller wheel. On the larger wheel, write word endings: at, in, ow, en, or, it—or other combinations.

Students turn the wheel to make three-letter words, then write the words on a piece of paper. At the end, students read their words and circle the ones that are not real.

28.

How Many Words Can You Make? Grades K – 2

Cut a number of large or jumbo puzzle pieces, half in blue and half in red. On the red pieces, along the bottom right, write either a consonant, blend or digraph. On the blue pieces, along the bottom left, write word endings (e.g., ay, at, ain, en, etty, air, ing, all, ut, een, awl, amp, in, ank, ell, ump, ill, ame, ick, ush).

In a center, students first separate the puzzle pieces by color, matching a red puzzle piece with a blue one to make a word. Students write the words they make on a paper to be checked later by the teacher.

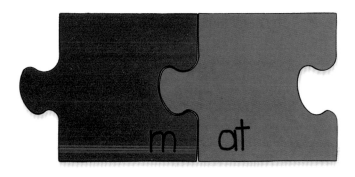

29.

Vocabulary Bingo   Grades K – 2

Cut enough bingo cards for each student in your class. Print a high frequency word in each square and cover the center square with a sticker. Students cover the words with tokens as the teacher calls them out randomly. Students try to cover five squares in a row horizontally, vertically or diagonally.

Ideas

Here are a couple of other ways to play this game!

- Write single letters in the spaces, then say a word that begins with one of the letters.
- Use only vowels on the card. Students cover a vowel the teacher sounds out (a,e,i,o,u—long or short), then names it.

30.

Stoplight Word Game   Grades K – 2

Cut several Puzzle #8 pieces from red, yellow and green construction paper. Write initial consonants on the green pieces, middle vowels on yellow pieces, and final consonants on red pieces. Children can play in pairs or small groups. Students turn all the pieces over, then take turns picking up three pieces: one green, one yellow and one red. Putting the letters together, they read the word. If they can pronounce it and it is a real word, they get two points. If it is a nonsense word, they get one point. The student with the most points at the end of the game wins.

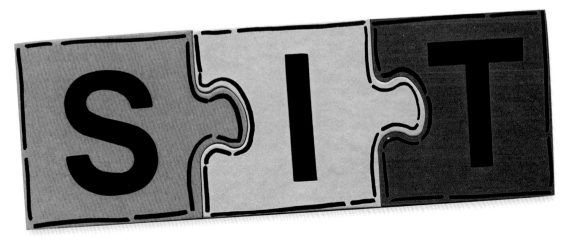

31.

Colored Pencils Grades K – 1

Create a set of colored die-cut pencils, along with index cards or pieces of cardstock on which you have written matching color words. Cut pencil shapes in red, blue, orange, purple, black, white, yellow and green. On the back of each pencil, write the color word to match the color of the pencil. Place pencils and index cards into a Bag #1 die cut.

Students in a center match the pencils with the color words. They turn the pencils over to check the answers.

Back

Colored Pencil Card Game

Red

Front

32.

Visual Discrimination Activity Grades Pre-K – K

Cut out a jumbo gingerbread house and 12 large die-cut gingerbread boys. Attach the gingerbread house to the front of a medium-sized gift bag.

Decorate pairs of gingerbread boys to match each other. To distinguish the pairs from one another, vary the types of eyes, smiles and bow ties, and the number of buttons.

Students take all of the gingerbread boys out of the bag and match the ones that are the same.

Gingerbread Boy Matching

33.

Pigs In the Pigpen

Grades Pre-K – K

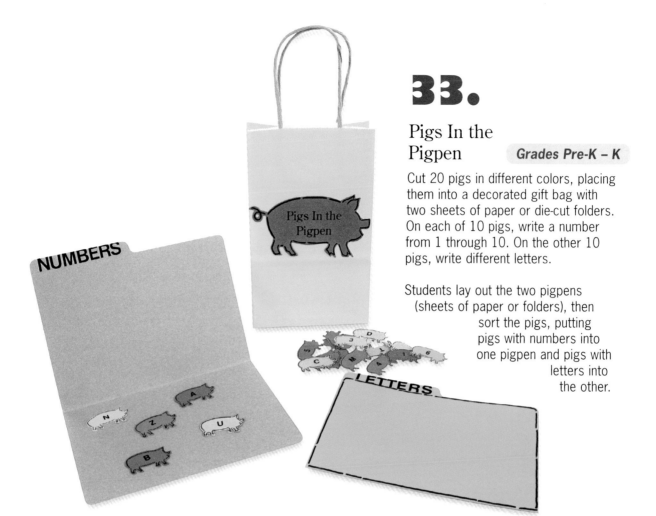

Cut 20 pigs in different colors, placing them into a decorated gift bag with two sheets of paper or die-cut folders. On each of 10 pigs, write a number from 1 through 10. On the other 10 pigs, write different letters.

Students lay out the two pigpens (sheets of paper or folders), then sort the pigs, putting pigs with numbers into one pigpen and pigs with letters into the other.

34.

Letter-Matching Apples

Grades Pre-K – K

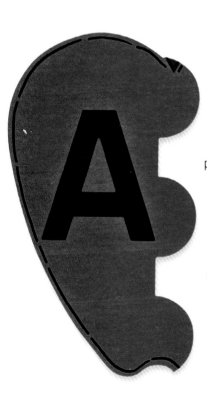

Cut 26 jumbo apples from construction paper: nine red, nine green, eight yellow. Using a simple border die design, such as Border-Scallop or Border-Jigsaw, place the jumbo apples lengthwise onto the border die, so the blade cuts the apples in two down the middle. Cut apples at different angles on the border die to make 26 unique puzzles. This ensures that students make a correct match. On half of each apple, write an uppercase letter. On the other half, write the corresponding lowercase letter. Students mix up the apple puzzle pieces and practice matching uppercase and lowercase letters.

35.

Taking Turns Grades Pre-K – 3

This idea helps students practice oral reading and fluency. Write each student's name on a large die-cut shape, such as a frog. Choose die cuts from a basket or bag to decide which student to call on for reading or answering questions. As you call on students, put each frog to the side so everyone gets a chance. At the end of the day, put all of the frogs back into the basket or bag.

Use this method to call on students to run errands or to be "it" in outdoor games.

36.

Theme Boxes Grades Pre-K – 3

Decorate large book storage boxes with jumbo die cuts in themes (e.g., jumbo pig die cut for books about pigs, penguins for books about penguins). Fill the boxes with books relating to the theme.

37.

Sight Word Bingo Grades K – 3

Cut enough bingo cards for each student in the class. Using a black thin-tip marker, write Dolch sight words in each square, varying the location from card to card. On each of a number of small die-cut shapes, write a word and a bingo letter. The bingo "caller" uses these die cuts to call. The winner is the first student to identify and cover five squares in a row horizontally, vertically or diagonally.

Hint

AccuCut offers several shaped bingo cards that coordinate with holidays or seasons (e.g., apple, flower, heart, pumpkin, mitten).

38.

The Long and Short of It

Grades 1 – 2

Cut five jumbo gingerbread houses. Along the roofline of one of the houses, write "Short I – Long I." Within the house sections, write words that include long "i" and short "i" sounds.

Ask students to draw a line down the middle of a piece of paper, creating two columns. Ask them to write "Short I" at the top of one column and "Long I" above the other. Show students the words on the house. Give them time to list all of the words, each on the correct half of the paper. Use the other four gingerbread houses to teach the other vowel sounds.

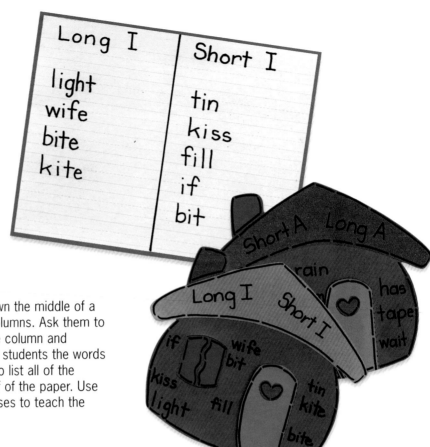

Long I	Short I
light	tin
wife	kiss
bite	fill
kite	if
	bit

39.

Cans of Learning

Grades Pre-K – 3

Cover a potato chip can with contact paper. Choose a theme, and glue a title relating to the theme onto the front of the can. For example, if you choose fish, choose a title such as "Going Fishing." Cut 26 mini die-cut fish in different colors, and write the letters of the alphabet on the fish. Put capital letters on one side and lowercase letters on the other.

Students pour the fish out of the can and put them in ABC order using capital letters. When they are finished, they scramble the letters and start again, this time putting the lowercase letters in order.

Front

Back

40.

What's the First Letter? Grades 1 – 2

Cut a set of large die cuts in a variety of shapes (e.g., star, pig, hand, apple). Glue each die cut onto a large 5" x 8" index card. On the card, write the word that matches the die-cut shape, but draw a blank where the first letter of each word would be. For example: __pple, __ig, and so on. On the backs of the index cards, write the missing letters so students can check their work.

41.

Read with Your Hands Grades 1 – 2

Cut out 10 jumbo hands. On each one, across the back of the hand, write a word ending such as: ate, ish, ipe or eat. On the end of each finger, write a consonant such as f, g, t, p or r.

On a piece of paper, students write the words they can make using the first letter and the word endings. They say the words, circling the ones that are not words.

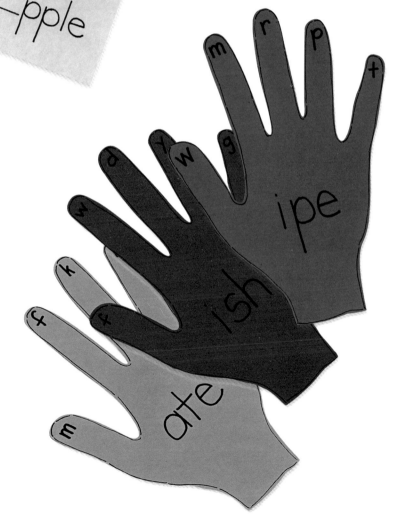

42.

Frogs In the Pond   Grades K – 3

Cut out about 20 large die-cut frogs. Write words or letters on each set of die-cut frogs so they match (see list of ideas). Make enough frogs so each student can have one. Use a Basket #7 die cut to create a frog pond. Place frogs in the pond, and let each student pick a frog.

When every student has a frog, ask students to walk silently around the room checking other frogs until they find a match. When they find a match, both students return frogs to the pond, then return to their seats.

Ideas

Use die-cut frogs to teach these concepts:

- Contractions
- Number words/numerals
- Rhyming words
- Singular/plural

- Compound words
- Number words/number of dots
- Vocabulary words/meanings

43.

Paired Reading   Grades 1 – 3

Ask students to write their names on either a jumbo die-cut boy shape or a jumbo die-cut girl shape. Place the girl and boy die cuts into a bucket. When it's time to choose a partner for paired reading or games, ask students to pull out die cuts to find their partners.

Choose girl and boy die cuts from a bucket when you want to call on students randomly to answer questions, run errands or read.

44.

Letter and Word Machines   *Grades K – 3*

Create letter and word machines with jumbo die cuts, such as the Fish #1 shape. Near the tail of each fish, using a craft knife or box cutter, cut a slit about three inches long. The fish already has a gill slit behind the eyes. Next, cut a piece of adding machine tape about 2½ feet long. Thread the tape from the back of the fish, up through the slit by the tail. Pull the tape across the length of the body, and thread it from the front down through the gill. You can glue the two ends of the adding machine tape together to make a circular strip.

With a marker, write letters or words on the part of the strip that shows on the fish's front. Students pull on the tape to see the next word to read. If you like, allow students to create their own machines after you have cut the slit in the jumbo die. If you want to make the machines reusable for other skills, don't glue the ends of the adding machine tape. You can pull out the strip and put in a different one.

Ideas

Use die-cut shape machines like this fish to teach these concepts:

- Word families
- Contractions/parts of contractions
- Proper nouns/common nouns
- Problem solving

- Long vowel/short vowel words
- Addition, subtraction or multiplication problems

45.

Don't Bug Me
—I'm Reading! *Grades Pre-K – 3*

Create door hangers for students, or allow them to make their own. One idea is to cut a door hanger for each student and ask students to write this saying on the front: "Don't Bug Me—I'm Reading!" Cut mini insects in bright colors and glue them around the words.

Ideas

Use door hangers to display these other sayings and mini die-cut decorations:

- "I Would Drive a Mile for a Good Book." (mini cars)
- "Leaf Me Alone. I'm Reading." (mini leaves)
- "Reading Makes Me Happy."
- "Walk Through the Pages of a Good Book." (mini feet)

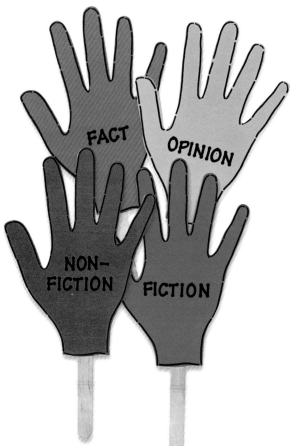

46.

The Hands Have It *Grades 2 – 5*

Cut two jumbo hands for each student. Have students glue two Hand #1 die cuts together, sandwiching a tongue depressor between them. Students write "Fact" on one side of the hand and "Opinion" on the other side of the hand. The teacher asks questions, and students hold up their "hands" to answer the questions.

Ideas

Use hands glued to tongue depressors to teach the following concepts, too. Write one item on one side of the hand, and the other item on the other side.

- Fiction/non-fiction
- Cause/effect
- True/False

47.

Story Mobiles   *Grades 1 – 5*

Ask each student to create a mobile illustrating a story the class is reading together. Provide pre-cut die cuts to illustrate the story. For example, for *Charlotte's Web* by E.B. White, cut out pigs, spiders and spider webs.

To make the mobiles, students can use a 3-D spiral die cut or punch three holes in a strip of cardstock. Punch a single hole in each of the die cuts. Show students how to attach the pig, spider and web to the spiral or cardstock strip using eight-inch lengths of yarn. Ask students to write the title of the book on the mobile or use a Web die cut to list title, characters, plot, setting or other points of interest in the book.

Hint

Ask second and third graders to write words or sentences about the story on both sides of small index cards, then hang the cards from mobiles.

Front

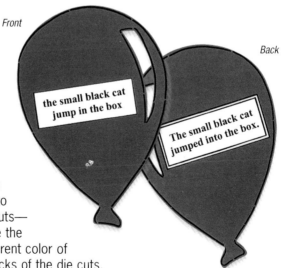

Back

the small black cat jump in the box

The small black cat jumped into the box.

48.

Correct the Mistakes   *Grades 2 – 3*

Print or type several sentences with mistakes in them on white paper. Cut the sentences into strips and attach to the fronts of jumbo die cuts—Balloon #1 shapes, for example. Print or type the corrected sentences on a different color of paper and attach to the backs of the die cuts.

Students turn all the balloons over so only the sentences printed on white paper show. Each student chooses a balloon and looks at the sentence with mistakes. He or she rewrites the sentence correctly on a piece of paper, then turns over the balloon and checks to see if they rewrote the sentence correctly. The student circles any mistakes on the paper using a crayon.

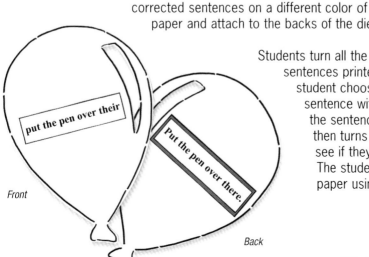

put the pen over their

Put the pen over there.

Front

Back

49.

Board Game   *Grades 1 – 3*

Glue the die-cut game board on a large piece of construction paper. Attach a small spinner on one side. Write the words "Start" and "Finish" on either end of the game board.

Students make their own board games, decorating them with stickers, drawings or mini die cuts. The teacher creates question cards to go with the games. For first graders, play games in small groups with the teacher. To play, students take turns choosing sight words from the question cards and saying the words. If they read the words correctly, they spin to see how many spaces to move.

Comprehension Is the Name of the Game   **Grades 2 – 3**

Cut 10 die-cut jumbo turtles. On each turtle, write a comprehension question from a story the class is reading. On the reverse side of the turtle, write the answer. With a partner, each student chooses a turtle, reads the question, then answers the question. If the answer is correct, the student gets to keep the turtle. The winner is the person with the most turtles after 10 questions have been answered.

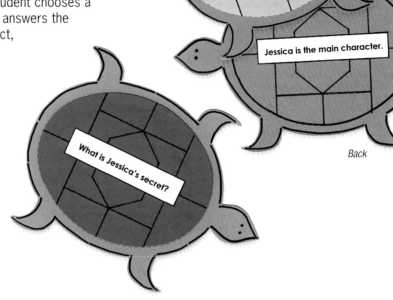

Front

Who is the main character of the story?

Jessica is the main character.

What is Jessica's secret?

Back

Front

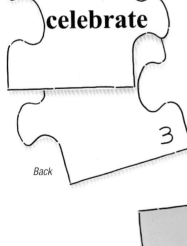

celebrate

3

Back

51.

Syllable Puzzle   **Grades 2 – 4**

Cut 20 puzzle pieces, and write one-, two-, three- or four-syllable words on them. On the reverse side of each puzzle piece, write the number of syllables.

In a center, two students turn over all the puzzle pieces so the words are showing. Each student chooses a word, reads the word, and says how many syllables are in that word. If they are correct, they earn their first piece of the puzzle. Students take turns answering the questions. The winner is the student with the most puzzle pieces at the end of the game. If a student cannot read a word, another student may help.

ocean

mother

house

100 Great Literacy Ideas Using AccuCut® Dies

52.

Looking for Plurals   Grades 2 – 3

On the cover of a pocket file folder, glue a pair of glasses frames and write the title of the pocket folder game: "Looking for Plurals." On the left pocket, write the word "Singular". On the right pocket, write the word "Plural". On index cards or another die-cut shape, write singular words. On another set of index cards or shapes, write plural words. Put the cards into the proper pockets with an answer key to help students check their work.

Students take the index cards out of the pockets and match each singular word with its plural form, then they check the answer sheet.

For example:
- City – Cities
- Ox – Oxen
- Goose – Geese
- Loaf – Loaves
- Man – Men
- Woman – Women
- Leaf – Leaves
- Berry – Berries
- Mouse – Mice
- Chair – Chairs
- Hero – Heroes
- Tooth – Teeth
- Glass – Glasses
- Potato – Potatoes

Idea

Use this activity to teach many different matching games by changing the title and pocket categories.

53.

Handwriting Practice

Cut a number of jumbo pencils from light colors of paper. On the pencils, print letters, students' names, days of the week, months or sentences you want students to practice writing.

Each student chooses a pencil, then copies the letters, words or sentences on paper. Use this activity to give older students practice in writing cursive and spelling.

54.

Choose a Category

Grades 1 – 3

Cut out jumbo die cuts whose shapes represent different categories, such as flowers (tulip), land animals (dog), transportation (car), water animals (fish), farm animals (pig) and so on. Write the category on each die cut. Choose a category, and ask students to brainstorm a list in that category. Students brainstorm as many things as possible that fit into the category. Write each word on the board, and keep track of the number of words. On another day, the class can try to beat their score with another category.

Later, use these category die cuts and words in a center. Write each word from two or three categories on an index card. Put the word cards into the center, along with coordinating category shapes. The student lays category shapes at the top, placing each card into the correct category.

Idea

Use the word cards from this activity to teach spelling words and writing activities, too—or use them to create a theme word wall.

55.

Fishing for Words Grades 1 – 2

Divide the class into groups of three or four for this game, or prepare the game for students to play in a center. First, cut out a number of jumbo fish. On each fish, write a word family. One student chooses a jumbo fish out of a bag to identify the word family for the next round of the game.

Students in their groups write as many real words in that word family as they can. When the teacher says, "Pencils down," each team reports the number of words they have found. Ask each team to read their words to find out which team has the most. In a center, students can play each other.

Some word families:

- ight
- ill
- in
- ing
- ink
- ack
- ame
- ash
- ate
- ish
- ap
- ay
- est
- ell
- eat
- ore
- op
- ock
- ide
- aw
- oke
- ug
- uck
- ump

Words that can be made from "ight", for example, include: fight, light, sight, might, night, right, tight, slight, fright, bright, flight, blight.

56.

Can You Comprehend?

Grades 2 – 3

After reading a story, ask students to use complete sentences to create questions other students can answer. Students write the questions on the fronts of the jumbo cars and their names on the backs of the cars.

When students are finished writing questions and names, collect all the cars and choose questions to ask the class. Later, put the questions into a center for students to read, and ask them to write answers to the questions in complete sentences.

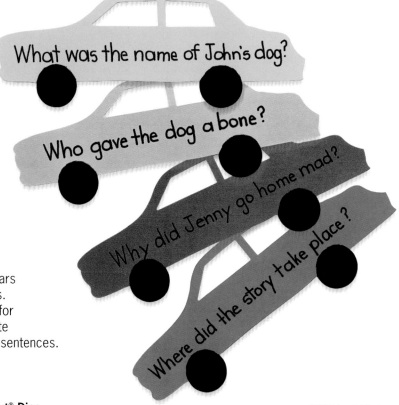

Short Vowels

57.

Shape Pockets *Grades 1 – 2*

This is a great center activity! Fold two paper plates or jumbo die-cut circles in half, and staple or glue the sides to make pockets. Cut out shapes whose names begin with long and short vowel sounds. Write "Short Vowels" on one paper plate pocket, and "Long Vowels" on the other. Students go through the shapes and sort them into the correct pockets.

Idea

For more of a challenge, cut shapes whose names include the vowel sound in the middle of the word. Write answers on the backs of the shapes so students who are able to read can check their answers.

AccuCut offers a die set for the long vowel and short vowel sounds. The long vowel set includes: acorn, eagle, ice cream cone, overalls and United States. The short vowel set includes: apple, egg, igloo, octopus and umbrella.

Long Vowels

58.

Star Reader Awards `Grades K – 3`

To encourage independent reading, give students award magnets to take home. Cut star shapes from flexible magnetic sheets in yellow, red and blue. Students receive a yellow star after they read five books, a red star after 10 books and a blue star for 15 books. The number of books can be adjusted to fit your classroom goals. The same idea works to reward achievements in spelling, math and other subjects.

59.

Words to Remember Bookmarks

`Grades 1 – 5`

Give each student a bookmark he or she can use to list new words they encounter in reading. This list of unfamiliar words may also be used as a spelling list.

For upper grades, make the bookmarks into booklets so students can write more words. To make the booklets, first fold a piece of construction paper in half. Place the fold inside the blade on the right side of the Bookmark-Generic #3 die and cut. Cut lined paper with the same bookmark die, and fasten inside the bookmark booklet with a brad.

60.

Grab Bag Spelling   Grades 2 – 4

Decorate a gift bag with die-cut shapes, and put the bag into a center. Write one spelling word on a seasonal die-cut shape, such as a heart. Taking turns with a partner, one student says the word, and the other student spells it. When a student spells a word wrong, he or she should write it on a Words to Remember bookmark (see Idea #59) to study that night. This also is a good way to practice past spelling words.

Elna inherits money from Great-aunt Edith.

Rancher Hicks has lunch at Millie's luncheonette.

Elna strikes oil!

61.

Story Sequence Puzzles   Grades 1 – 4

List the main events in a reading story on puzzle pieces. Scramble the pieces. Individually or in groups, students arrange the puzzle pieces into the correct order.

Ideas

Here are different ways to teach with story sequence puzzles:

- Students list the main events themselves, then they exchange puzzles with other students who arrange the pieces.
- Younger students can draw pictures of the story events on puzzle pieces.
- Glue separated newspaper cartoon panels to puzzle pieces to create another sequencing activity.

62.

Conversation Balloons

Grades 2 – 5

Cut enough colorful jumbo die-cut balloons for each student in your class. After studying proper punctuation, ask each student to write a sentence on the balloon, using his or her own name in the sentence (e.g., "Will I be next in line?" asked Jackie.). Put the balloons on a bulletin board to remind students to use proper punctuation.

63.

Fishbowl Synonyms and Antonyms

Grades 2 – 4

Laminate two sheets of blue construction paper, and cut out two jumbo fishbowls. Label one fishbowl "Synonyms" and the other "Antonyms". Cut out 20 small fish from cling vinyl material. Using a permanent marker, write pairs of synonyms or antonyms on the fish. The cling vinyl fish will stick to the laminated fishbowls. Students can work independently classifying word pairs in a center.

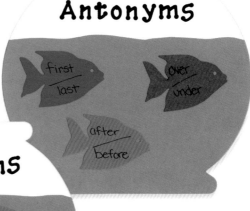

64.

Star Readers   *Grades 1 – 4*

Encourage independent reading! Cut out Folder-Slash pockets and label with each student's name. Post pockets on a "Star Readers" bulletin board. As students read books, they write titles and authors on die-cut stars and put them into their pockets.

Ideas

- Students can rate books they've read using a one-star through five-star rating system. Students look at other student's stars for recommendations on books to read.
- Make "star notes" to send home to parents. Use the shape card folding technique by folding paper in half and placing fold inside of blade on die at side of shape, then die cut.

65.

Sentence Cubes   *Grades 2 – 3*

Cut and assemble six die-cut cubes. Create six sentences made up of six words each to use in this activity. On self-adhesive labels, type each word from all the sentences. Adhere all of the words to the cubes, one word to each cube side.

In a center, students turn the cubes, choosing words until they find complete sentences that make sense. They write the sentences on a piece of paper, then try again using the cubes to make more sentences.

66.

Character Flip-Flaps Grades 2 – 3

Cut enough Flip-Flap #1 die cuts for each student in the class. Fold flaps over, and ask students to write names and illustrate story characters on each flap. They may illustrate the characters with a drawing or a die cut. Under each flap, they list three adjectives that describe that character.

67.

Vocabulary Mobile Grades 1 – 2

Use a jumbo shape to indicate a word category, such as a car for transportation or a house for shelter. Print the name of the category on the shape, then ask students to brainstorm related words. Students write the words on die cut cards and hang them from the jumbo shape. For example, write transportation on a car, then hang words from it, such as "airplane", "train", "bus", and "bicycle".

Idea

Use vocabulary from content area for older students (i.e., a biomes category would include: "desert", "tundra", and "rainforest").

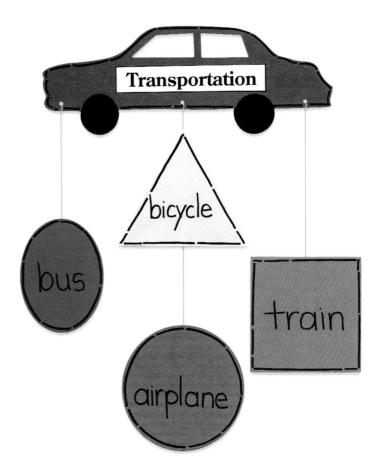

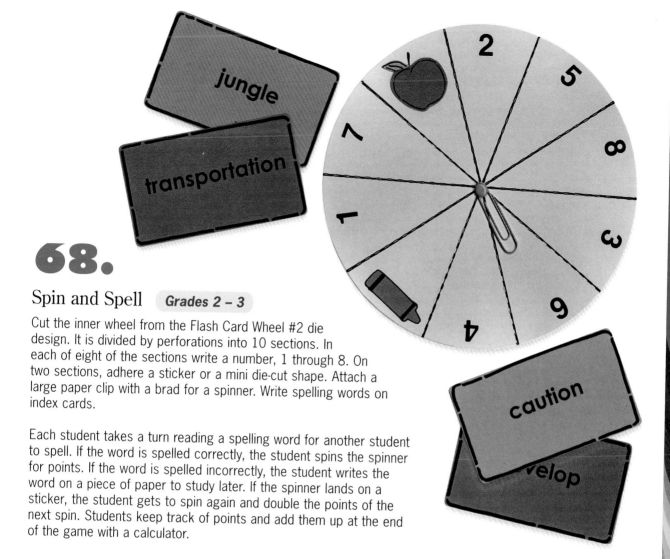

68.

Spin and Spell   Grades 2 – 3

Cut the inner wheel from the Flash Card Wheel #2 die design. It is divided by perforations into 10 sections. In each of eight of the sections write a number, 1 through 8. On two sections, adhere a sticker or a mini die-cut shape. Attach a large paper clip with a brad for a spinner. Write spelling words on index cards.

Each student takes a turn reading a spelling word for another student to spell. If the word is spelled correctly, the student spins the spinner for points. If the word is spelled incorrectly, the student writes the word on a piece of paper to study later. If the spinner lands on a sticker, the student gets to spin again and double the points of the next spin. Students keep track of points and add them up at the end of the game with a calculator.

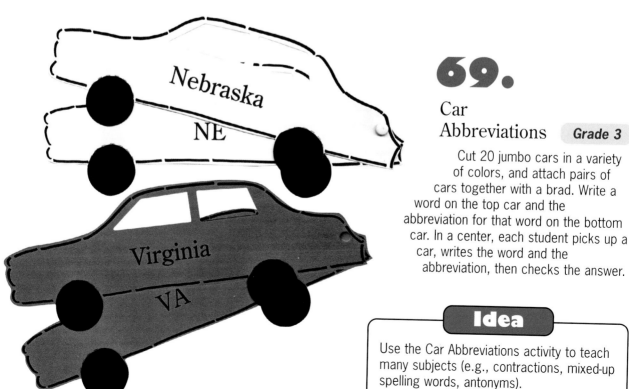

69.

Car Abbreviations   Grade 3

Cut 20 jumbo cars in a variety of colors, and attach pairs of cars together with a brad. Write a word on the top car and the abbreviation for that word on the bottom car. In a center, each student picks up a car, writes the word and the abbreviation, then checks the answer.

Idea

Use the Car Abbreviations activity to teach many subjects (e.g., contractions, mixed-up spelling words, antonyms).

70.

Apples with Worms   **Grades Pre-K – 3**

Cut 20 large or jumbo Apple with Worm shapes to create center activities. Students thread the worms through two slits in the matching apples. Create many different matching activities with the apples and worms.

Hint

For example:

- Capital letters/lowercase letters
- Contractions
- Singular/plural
- Vowel sounds
- Numbers/number words
- Colors/color words
- Numbers of syllables

Write answers on the backs of the apples so students can check their answers after they do the work.

71.

Let the Cat Out of the Bag   **Grades Pre-K – 3**

Cut 20 jumbo cats in a variety of colors and five cats in black. Leave the black cats blank, but write skills on the other 20 cats, such as:

- Historical facts
- Multiplication problems
- Color identification
- Number or color words
- Nouns or verbs
- True or false
- Animals and their habitats

Students take turns in a center pulling a cat out of the bag and saying the answer. Students get a point for every correct answer. Each turn ends when the student draws a black cat. The next student pulls a cat out of the bag. When finished, all the cats go back into the bag and the game starts again.

72.

Down On the Farm
Grades 2 – 3

Cut 20 mini farm animals for each student. Write a word on each animal. Ask students to put the words in alphabetical order. For third grade, include some words that begin with the same letter so that students will have to look at the second or even the third letter to alphabetize them. Print out the answers, so students can check their work.

Idea

Make a set of die-cut farm animals. On the die cuts, write the names of all the students in the class. Students have fun putting their own names in alphabetical order.

73.

Get Your Ducks In a Row
Grades Pre-K – 3

Cut three jumbo-size ducks and 21 large-size ducklings. On each jumbo duck, write a category. On each duckling, write words or glue pictures that fit into that category. Some ideas for using the ducks are:

- Nouns, verbs and adjectives
- Person, place or thing
- Plurals that end in s, es or ies

Idea

For younger students, cut only two jumbo ducks and 20 ducklings. Cut out pictures and glue them onto the ducks and ducklings. Ask students to sort the ducklings according to pictures of living and non-living items.

Back

Front

humid

74.

The Mouse and the Cheese   Grades 1 – 3

Front

dry

Back

Create a game with jumbo mouse and cheese die cuts. Cut 20 mice and 20 pieces of cheese. Write questions on the mice and answers on the cheese. Students turn over the mice and cheese, placing the writing-side down. They take turns throwing a die. If a student gets an even number, he or she gets a mouse. If a student rolls an odd number, he or she gets a piece of cheese. The object of the game is to match questions with answers and have the most matches at the end of the game. Students also may see if they have mice that match their opponents' cheese shapes. If so, they should check answers together.

Idea

Use The Mouse and the Cheese to teach these concepts, too:

- Rhyming words
- Antonyms
- Compound words
- Comprehension questions from a story
- Color words/colors
- Problem solving sentences
- Words with missing letters

75.

Feed the Dog *Grades 2 – 3*

Cut one Mask #3 shape and two dog ears and a nose shape from Mask #3 Accessories #2. Cut one paper plate in half, then staple to a whole paper plate to make a pocket. Glue the mask, ears and nose onto the entire paper plate. Write sentences on large bone die cuts—some of them true, some of them false.

Students draw bone cards from a stack and read them. They decide whether each sentence is true or false. If a sentence is true, the student "feeds" the bone to the dog. Use sentences from a story the students are reading, or general sentences such as, "Some dogs are green." or "Cats can stay underwater for hours."

Cats are from the feline family.

Dogs are carnivores.

Some dogs are green.

Cats have nine lives.

P.J. Smith

1. bugs
2. bullfrog

76.

Alphabetical Order *Grades 2 – 3*

Cut a number of jumbo animal shapes. On each shape, write words that have to do with that animal. Ask students to write the words on a piece of paper in alphabetical order.

frog leap
tadpoles pond
webbed toad
water bugs
bullfrog jump

100 Great Literacy Ideas Using AccuCut® Dies

77.

Filmstrip
Game Board Grades 3 – 5

Glue two filmstrip die cuts onto a 12" x 18" piece of construction paper.

To begin the activity, give each student a different-colored marker. One student picks up the top card, turns it over, says the word and decides if it is a noun, verb or adjective. If the first square on the board says "noun" and the student picks up a card with a noun, he or she places a marker on that square. If the student picks up a card with any word other than a noun, the student must put the card at the bottom of the deck, and the other person takes a card. If the square says "verb" and the card picked up says, "jump", the student would say, "verb", then move his or her marker to the next square on the game board. The game continues, with students trying to draw cards that match the next square on the board.

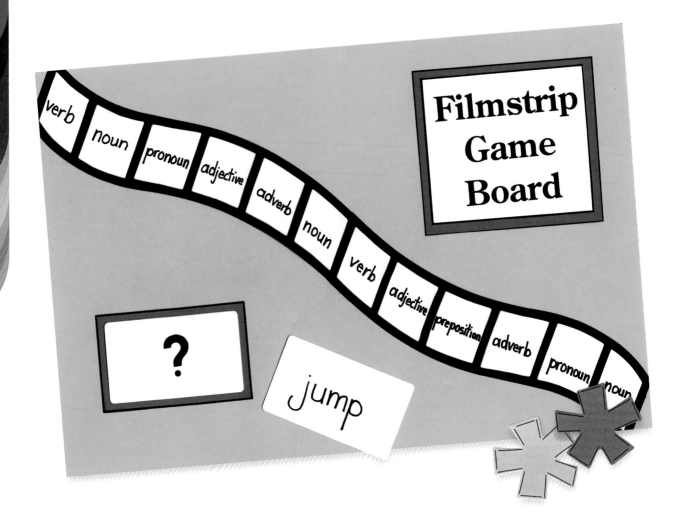

Idea

For younger students, write a consonant letter in each of the 12 squares of the filmstrip die cuts. Cut pictures of items whose names begin with the letters you put in each square and glue the pictures onto index cards.

Back

Front

78.

Vocabulary Practice

Grades 2 – 3

Cut out about 20 jumbo hands. On one side, write a vocabulary word. On the other side, write a short meaning.

Students place all the hands onto the table, word-side-up. One student reads a word and another student says the meaning, taking turns. A correct answer means the student gets the hand.

Idea

Use this activity to teach these concepts, too:

- Comprehension questions
- Spelling words
- Singular/plural
- Many other reading and language arts activities

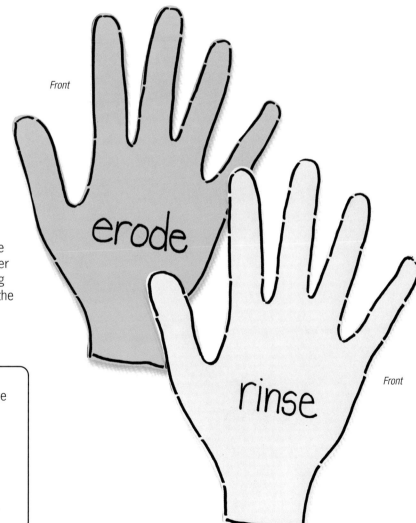

Front

Front

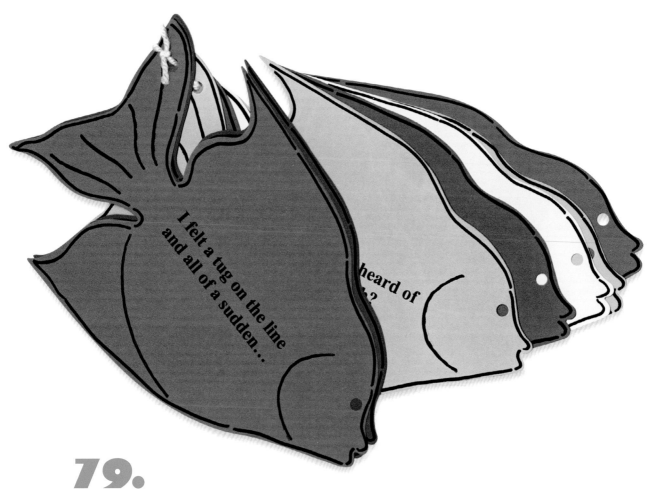

I felt a tug on the line and all of a sudden...

...heard of ...?

79.

A String of Fish   Grades 2 – 3

Cut 10 jumbo Fish #3 shapes from construction paper in a variety of colors. Punch a hole in the tail of each fish. Slip a piece of yarn approximately eight inches long through each of the holes. Tie the ends of the yarn together, creating a large loop.

On each fish, write a story starter students can use to write short stories. Students choose a story starter from the fish on the string and begin writing. The string of fish works well as a center activity.

Ideas

Write the following story starters on fish, or make up your own.

- I felt a tug on the line and all of a sudden...
- While in Tampa, Florida, I went fishing with...
- The biggest fish I ever caught was...
- I was looking into the jaws of a killer whale when...
- Have you ever heard of a talking fish? Well, I have.

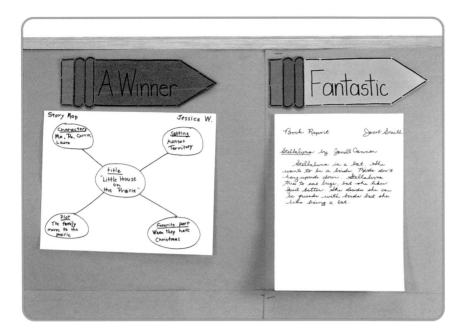

80.

Pencil Toppers Grades K – 5

To highlight students' writing work, use jumbo die-cut pencils. Attach pencils to the tops of students' writing papers and post them on the bulletin board. You can write each student's name on a pencil—or the words "Great", "Fantastic" or "A Winner".

Front

Back

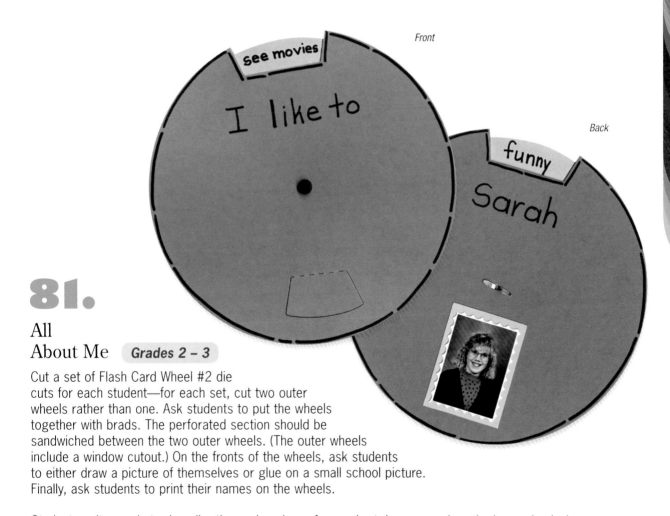

81.

All About Me Grades 2 – 3

Cut a set of Flash Card Wheel #2 die cuts for each student—for each set, cut two outer wheels rather than one. Ask students to put the wheels together with brads. The perforated section should be sandwiched between the two outer wheels. (The outer wheels include a window cutout.) On the fronts of the wheels, ask students to either draw a picture of themselves or glue on a small school picture. Finally, ask students to print their names on the wheels.

Students write words to describe themselves (e.g., funny, short, brown eyes) on the inner wheel where the words will show through the window cutouts on one side. They turn the wheel over, and on the reverse side they write words to show things they like to do (e.g., see movies, read, play soccer). Using the words on the wheel, students write a few paragraphs describing themselves. Another day, students can exchange wheels and write about another student.

100 Great Literacy Ideas Using AccuCut® Dies

82.

All-About-Me Booklet   Grades 2 – 3

Ask students to make booklets, with large folded sheets of construction paper as covers. On his or her cover, each student can glue the flash card wheel made in Idea #81, picture side up. Inside the booklet, ask students to glue writings about themselves. Around the flash card wheel on the construction paper, they can draw pictures of themselves or choose die cuts of things that show what they like to do (e.g., soccer ball, books, computer, bike).

Hint

The All-About-Me booklet can be an ongoing project in which students write journal entries throughout the year. Put extra paper into the booklet as needed.

83.

Pattern Block Story   Grades 2 – 3

Cut pattern block shapes in the same colors as wooden pattern blocks. Squares are orange, trapezoids are red, hexagons are yellow, parallelograms are white, rhombi are blue, and triangles are green. Students position these die-cut shapes together on a piece of black construction paper to make a picture of something or someone. Then they write a story to go along with the picture they made. Allow students to share pictures and stories or display them on a bulletin board.

Idea

Give students a topic, such as vehicles. Using pattern block shapes, students can make anything you can travel in such as trains, cars, hot air balloons or airplanes. As a class, graph the different types of vehicles students have created.

84.

Language Arts Puppets   Grades 2 – 3

Cut two of AccuCut's action figures, such as the pig and the cow, and ask students to assemble them with brads. Bring up a problem that the characters might have. An example may be that the pig is getting into the cow's food and the cow doesn't want to share. Put students into groups of two to work on the problem, using the action figures to stage a conversation between the two animals. Can they work out their problem?

Next, encourage students to brainstorm solutions and write them on the board. This could become a writing activity.

Ideas

Action figure puppets provide an effective method of working out solutions to students' problems, such as:

- Being picked on
- Feeling that nobody wants to play with them
- Making friends
- Making fun of other students
- Being a bully
- Lying
- Stealing
- Not doing homework

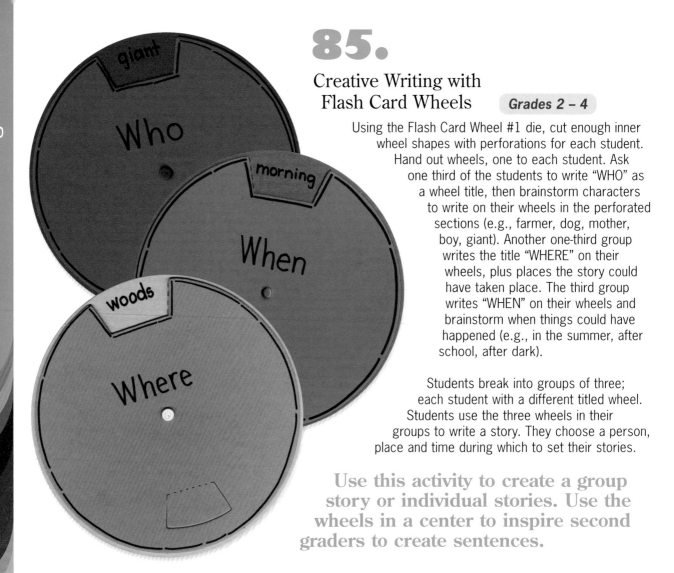

85.

Creative Writing with Flash Card Wheels Grades 2 – 4

Using the Flash Card Wheel #1 die, cut enough inner wheel shapes with perforations for each student. Hand out wheels, one to each student. Ask one third of the students to write "WHO" as a wheel title, then brainstorm characters to write on their wheels in the perforated sections (e.g., farmer, dog, mother, boy, giant). Another one-third group writes the title "WHERE" on their wheels, plus places the story could have taken place. The third group writes "WHEN" on their wheels and brainstorm when things could have happened (e.g., in the summer, after school, after dark).

Students break into groups of three; each student with a different titled wheel. Students use the three wheels in their groups to write a story. They choose a person, place and time during which to set their stories.

Use this activity to create a group story or individual stories. Use the wheels in a center to inspire second graders to create sentences.

86.

Pop-Up Book Report Grades 2 – 4

Students can add interest to written book reports by creating pop-up visual aids! Show them how to make a pop-up visual with die-cut shapes that relate to some aspect of the story. They may choose a shape to illustrate the main character, the setting or the plot line.

To create a pop-up visual, fold a piece of 9" x 12" construction paper in half. Attach a die-cut pop-up base inside, gluing the chosen die-cut shape to the pop-up. Each student can decorate his or her cover with a scene from the chosen story.

87.

Create a Story Problem ⟨Grades 2 – 5⟩

Cut a variety of large die-cut shapes and put the shapes in a colored gift bag or lunch sack. Write or type a title on the sack: "Create a Story Problem." At a math center, students pull out a shape and create a math story problem using that shape as the topic of their problem. They write their story problem on a piece of paper.

For example:
a) During the school basketball playoffs, five of the six teams brought 15 players. The sixth team brought only 12 players. How many players were there in all?

The teacher might want to assign students to create addition, subtraction or multiplication problems, and one-digit, two-digit or three-digit numbers. Students exchange and solve each other's problems. They can put answers on the backs, making the activity self-checking.

88.

Journal Writing ⟨Grades 1 – 3⟩

To encourage journal writing, ask students to write on a jumbo shape, or use a book die set, which includes a cover and an inside page for cutting lined writing paper. Students enjoy making their own books. They can add mini die-cut shapes to pages to add interest and color. Making the page more colorful encourages creative writing.

Idea

Here are shapes that work well for journal writing:

- Holiday shapes (Book-Pumpkin, Book-Heart)
- Sports (Book-Circle, T-shirt, pennant)
- Seasonal shapes (Book-Snowman, oak or maple leaves, Book-Flower)
- Pets (Dog #1, Cat #1, Horse #1)
- Memory book

89.

Flag Book Grades 2 – 5

Cut two sections of the flag book shape from white construction paper. Add lined paper inside, and staple the edges. Students color the flag book within the perforated lines, looking at the classroom's U.S. flag as a guide—or you may cut the cover from red, white and blue construction paper, then let students cut out the red stripes and blue box along the perforations and glue onto white flag.

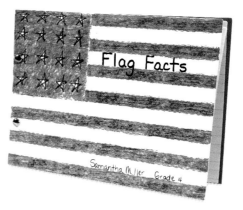

Idea

Inside of their flag books, students can write about a variety of topics. Here are a few examples:

- Election of the President
- Memorial Day
- Our country
- Dear Mr. President
- What I love about America
- Words to a patriotic song

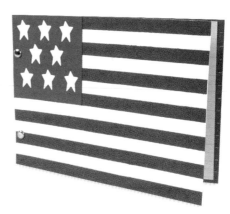

90.

Tangram Stories Grades 2 – 3

After reading *Grandfather Tang's Story* by Ann Tompert, give each student a set of tangram pieces and a piece of construction paper. Ask them to arrange the tangram pieces until they create pictures of animals or other objects they like. After creating their pictures, students may write short stories to go along with their designs.

Display these pictures and stories on a bulletin board, or put them together into a booklet to be shared in a center. Students also may check out the student-made tangram booklet to share with their families.

91.

Acrostic Name Poem Grades 2 – 4

Cut enough colorful jumbo die-cut balloons or other jumbo shapes to give one to each student in your class.

On the jumbo die cuts, ask students to write the letters of their names in capital letters, in a column. Then, across from each letter, they write two or three words to describe themselves. The first word should begin with the letter in their name.

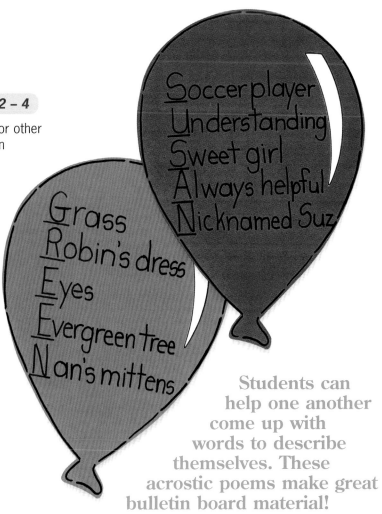

Grass
Robin's dress
Eyes
Evergreen tree
Nan's mittens

Soccer player
Understanding
Sweet girl
Always helpful
Nicknamed Suz

Hint

For first graders, write a color word (e.g., green) vertically on the shape. Let them work as a class to come up with green items whose names begin with each letter sound.

Students can help one another come up with words to describe themselves. These acrostic poems make great bulletin board material!

92.

Research Report Grades 3 – 5

Cut a variety of animal shapes and put them into a bag. Each student pulls out an animal, and that animal will be the subject of a report.

Take students to the library and let them look at books about the animals they chose. Each student checks out a book to read and makes notes on index cards. Students then write research reports about their animals, using their notes. They can use the die-cut animal shapes to decorate the covers of their reports.

93.

Story Map In the Round

Cut out a die-cut Puzzle #5 set for each student. Ask students to write the title of a story on the centerpiece, and story elements on the edge pieces (e.g., author, plot, characters, setting). Students may decorate this graphic organizer with die cuts or drawings.

94.

T-Shirt Writing   Grades 2 – 3

Cut enough jumbo T-shirt shapes in a variety of colors so each student in the class has one. Ask students to print their names in the centers of the T-shirts with a black crayon. Then, with a pencil, each student should write words that describe himself or herself.

Use the T-shirts as prompts for students to write a few paragraphs about themselves. Attach their paragraphs to the bottoms of the T-shirts, and display on the wall or on a clothesline.

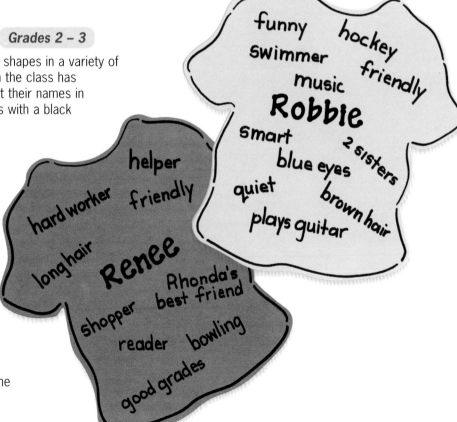

95.

Let's Talk   *Grades 2 – 3*

Cut a number of die-cut Border-Children #2 shapes. Each die-cut border includes five different children in a row. Cut apart the individual children. Students may pick two of the children to color and glue to the tops of their papers. Have them write a name below each die cut.

Each student writes a conversation between the two children on the paper, using proper punctuation and a new paragraph each time a different character is speaking.

Jacob

Ann

"Where are you going?" asked Ann.

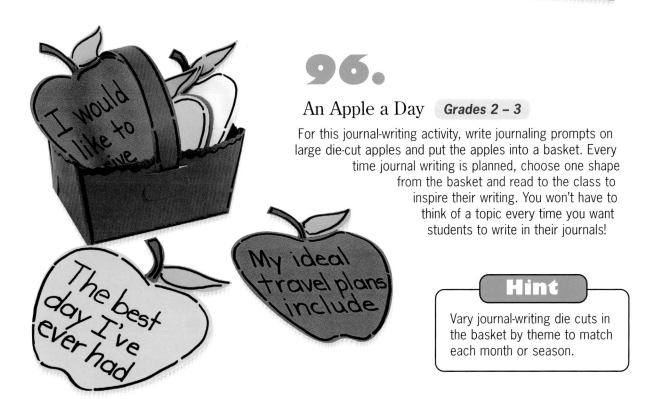

96.

An Apple a Day   *Grades 2 – 3*

For this journal-writing activity, write journaling prompts on large die-cut apples and put the apples into a basket. Every time journal writing is planned, choose one shape from the basket and read to the class to inspire their writing. You won't have to think of a topic every time you want students to write in their journals!

I would like to give

The best day I've ever had

My ideal travel plans include

Hint

Vary journal-writing die cuts in the basket by theme to match each month or season.

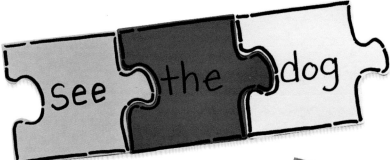

97.

Puzzle Piece Word Bank   Grades K – 2

Cut one Folder-Slash pocket for each student in the class. Ask each student to label the pocket with his or her name. As students learn new words, they copy the words onto small puzzle pieces and store the pieces in their slash folder pockets.

Hint

To practice writing skills, students can arrange puzzle words into sentences, and copy them onto paper using correct capitalization and punctuation.

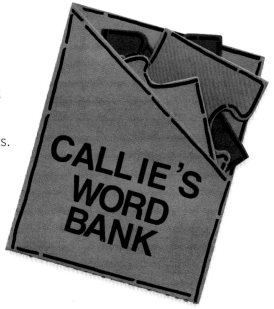

98.

Writing Portfolios   Grades 1 – 5

Cut out a variety of different shapes and colors, or use die cuts left over from other projects. Give each student a file folder for storing all of his or her writing projects, and allow students to decorate the folder with the die cuts. Students write his or her name on the front of their portfolios in large letters.

Idea

Store portfolios in a container in the classroom. Ask students to get their portfolios from the container when they are going to share their writing or store another project. Writing portfolios are effective for parent conferences, too.

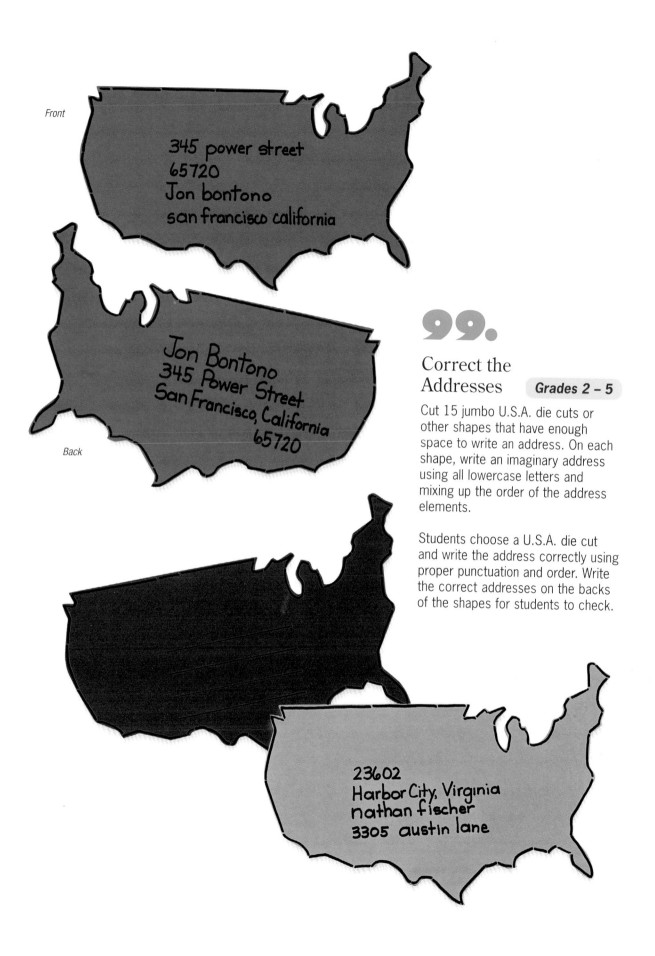

Front

345 power street
65720
Jon bontono
san francisco california

Back

Jon Bontono
345 Power Street
San Francisco, California
65720

99.

Correct the Addresses

Grades 2 – 5

Cut 15 jumbo U.S.A. die cuts or other shapes that have enough space to write an address. On each shape, write an imaginary address using all lowercase letters and mixing up the order of the address elements.

Students choose a U.S.A. die cut and write the address correctly using proper punctuation and order. Write the correct addresses on the backs of the shapes for students to check.

23602
Harbor City, Virginia
nathan fischer
3305 austin lane

100.

Create a Story   Grades 1 – 4

Cut a variety of animals to use as story characters. Students, in pairs. choose two characters for a story and brainstorm about the subject of their story. Then, using their characters, they write a story on the computer.

Student partners use a large piece of construction paper folded in half for the cover of their booklet. They put their story inside and staple the folded edge. The students use the die-cut animals and crayons to design a cover for their booklet.